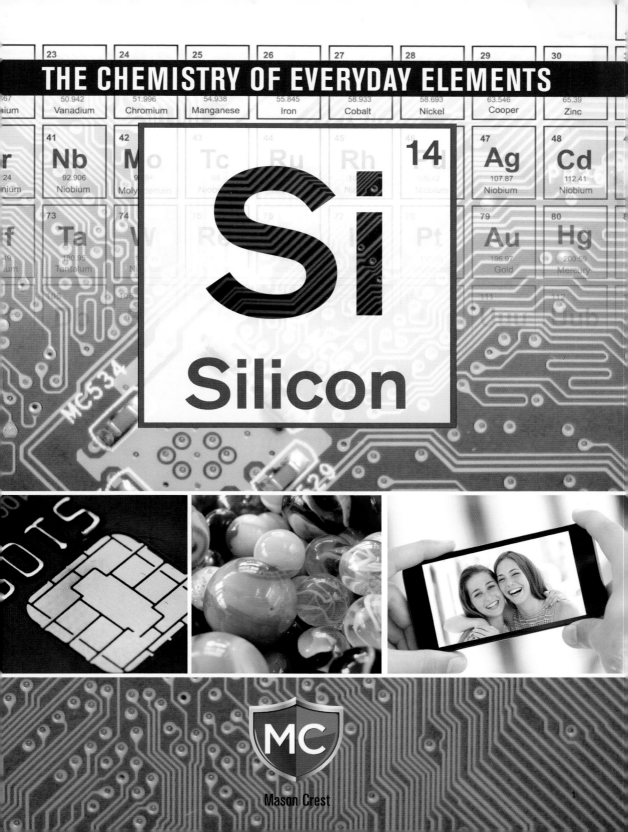

THE CHEMISTRY OF EVERYDAY ELEMENTS

23	24	25	26	27	28	29	30
50.942 Vanadium	51.996 Chromium	54.938 Manganese	55.845 Iron	58.933 Cobalt	58.693 Nickel	63.546 Cooper	65.39 Zinc

Si

14

Silicon

Mason Crest

THE CHEMISTRY OF EVERYDAY ELEMENTS

Si

14

Silicon

By Jane P. Gardner

Mason Crest
450 Parkway Drive, Suite D
Broomall, PA 19008
www.masoncrest.com

Series ISBN: 978-1-4222-3837-0
Hardback ISBN: 978-1-4222-3844-8
EBook ISBN: 978-1-4222-7949-6

First printing
1 3 5 7 9 8 6 4 2

Produced by Shoreline Publishing Group LLC
Santa Barbara, California
Editorial Director: James Buckley Jr.
Designer: Patty Kelley
www.shorelinepublishing.com

Library of Congress Cataloging-in-Publication Data on file with the Publisher.

Cover photographs by Dreamstime.com: Shuttlecock (left); Antonio Guillem (right); Arnis Rukis (bkgd). Wikimedia/Joe Mabel (center).

QR Codes disclaimer:

KEY ICONS TO LOOK FOR

Words to Understand: These words with their easy-to-understand definitions will increase the reader's understanding of the text, while building vocabulary skills.

Sidebars: This boxed material within the main text allows readers to build knowledge, gain insights, explore possibilities, and broaden their perspectives by weaving together additional information to provide realistic and holistic perspectives.

Educational Videos: Readers can view videos by scanning our QR codes, providing them with additional educational content to supplement the text. Examples include news coverage, moments in history, speeches, iconic moments, and much more!

Text-Dependent Questions: These questions send the reader back to the text for more careful attention to the evidence presented here.

Research Projects: Readers are pointed toward areas of further inquiry connected to each chapter. Suggestions are provided for projects that encourage deeper research and analysis.

Series Glossary of Key Terms: This back-of-the-book glossary contains terminology used throughout this series. Words found here increase the reader's ability to read and comprehend higher-level books and articles in this field.

Introduction

Take a close look around you. What do you see? A wall, a cat, a book, yesterday's lunch dishes. Outside your window, you might see clouds or rain or the sun shining while your heart pumps your blood throughout your body. All of those things—the solids, liquids, and gases around you—are composed of elements of the periodic table.

The periodic table is an arrangement of all the naturally occurring, and manufactured, elements known to humans at this point. There are 92 elements that can be found naturally on Earth and in space. The remaining 26 (and counting) have been manufactured and analyzed in a lab. These elements, alone or in combination with others, form and shape all the matter around us. From the air we breathe, to the water we drink, to the food we eat—all these things are made of elements.

A lot of information about an element can be learned just by finding its location on the periodic table. The periodic table

Elements play a part in everything in this photo, from clothes to leaves to people!

has undergone several updates and reorganizations since it was first developed in 1869. In the modern version of the table used today, it is arranged by increasing atomic number, into rows and columns. Each element has a unique atomic number. It is the number of protons in the nucleus of the atom. For example, uranium has an atomic number of 92—there are 92 protons in the nucleus. Hydrogen, on the other hand, has only one. All samples of an element have the same number of protons, but they may have a different number of neutrons in the nucleus. Atoms with the same number of protons but different number of neutrons are called isotopes. Certain chemical properties can be interpreted based on which group or row an element resides in. Each element on the periodic table is unique, having its own chemical and physical properties. The periodic table also gives important information such as the number of protons and neutrons in the nucleus of one atom of an element, the number of electrons that surround the nucleus, the atomic mass, and the general size of the atom. A symbol that is made up of one or two (or, in a few cases, three) letters represents the element. It is also possible to predict which state of matter—solid, liquid, or gas—an element is most likely to be found based on its location. The periodic table is a very useful tool as one begins to investigate chemistry and science in general.

Count 'em up: This diagram shows the 14 electrons of a silicon atom.

This book is about the element silicon. Silicon is number 14 on the periodic table. Minerals that contain the mineral silicon make up more than 90 percent of Earth's crust. Silicon is therefore the second most

Periodic Table

Period	Group 1	2	3	4	5	6	7	8	9	10	11	12	13	14	15	16	17	18
1	1 H																	2 He
2	3 Li	4 Be											5 B	6 C	7 N	8 O	9 F	10 Ne
3	11 Na	12 Mg											13 Al	14 Si	15 P	16 S	17 Cl	18 Ar
4	19 K	20 Ca	21 Sc	22 Ti	23 V	24 Cr	25 Mn	26 Fe	27 Co	28 Ni	29 Cu	30 Zn	31 Ga	32 Ge	33 As	34 Se	35 Br	36 Kr
5	37 Rb	38 Sr	39 Y	40 Zr	41 Nb	42 Mo	43 Tc	44 Ru	45 Rh	46 Pd	47 Ag	48 Cd	49 In	50 Sn	51 Sb	52 Te	53 I	54 Xe
6	55 Cs	56 Ba	57-71	72 Hf	73 Ta	74 W	75 Re	76 Os	77 Ir	78 Pt	79 Au	80 Hg	81 Tl	82 Pb	83 Bi	84 Po	85 At	86 Rn
7	87 Fr	88 Ra	89-103	104 Rf	105 Db	106 Sg	107 Bh	108 Hs	109 Mt	110 Ds	111 Rg	112 Cn	113 Uut	114 Uuq	115 Uup	116 Uuh	117 Uus	118 Uuo

6	57 La	58 Ce	59 Pr	60 Nd	61 Pm	62 Sm	63 Eu	64 Gd	65 Tb	66 Dy	67 Ho	68 Er	69 Tm	70 Yb	71 Lu
7	89 Ac	90 Th	91 Pa	92 U	93 Np	94 Pu	95 Am	96 Cm	97 Bk	98 Cf	99 Es	100 Fm	101 Md	102 No	103 Lr

The Periodic Table of the Elements is arranged in numerical order. The number of each element is determined by the number of protons in its nucleus. The horizontal rows are called periods. The number of the elements increases across a period, from left to right. The vertical columns are called groups. Groups of elements share similar characteristics. The colors, which can vary depending on the way the creators design their version of the chart, also create related collections of elements, such as noble gases, metals, or nonmetals, among others.

Si 14

Silicon

abundant element in the crust, second only to oxygen. In its pure form, silicon is a hard and brittle solid with a shiny blueish-gray color. However, silicon is rarely found on Earth in its pure form. Instead, it forms compounds that become minerals such as quartz. Quartz exists in a number of colors, including pink, clear, gray, purple, and white.

Silicon is all around us. It is used in the building materials that make up our homes and businesses, it is found in all our electronic

Quartz is made mostly of silicon; other elements or minerals provide colors.

devices, in bakeware and cosmetics, it is part of our diet, and is even found in sand castles on the beach. Read on to learn more about how silicon is used in electronics and solar panels, and how the famous Silicon Valley in California earned its name. Find out more about how silicon was discovered, if it exists on other planets or beyond, and whether or not alien life is silicon-based. Plus, find out the connection between three substances that are often confused: silica, silicon, and silicone.

Si ¹⁴
Silicon

WORDS TO UNDERSTAND

flint a hard form of the mineral quartz that is found in sedimentary rocks; also known as chert

hydrated containing added water

meteorite a meteor that passes through Earth's atmosphere and strikes the surface

Discovery and History

Silicon is the second most abundant element in Earth's crust. It makes up the majority of the beach sand in the world. We use it in soaps, in glass, and in computers. Historically, humans have been using, and even manipulating, silicon for thousands of years. Some of the very first tools made by early humans were made of **flint**, a form of the mineral quartz. Quartz is composed of atoms of silicon and oxygen. Flint easily breaks into thin shards or splinters, making it very useful to early humans during the Stone Age as tools or cutting instruments, or to start a fire. Early civilizations eventually learned to turn sand, which is composed primarily of silicon, into glass by heating it. Silicon was a vital piece of early human civilizations, but it did not have a name.

Silicon

Separating Silicon

Because silicon is so prevalent in our lives, and in the rocks all around us, it is difficult to think of it as something that needed to be "discovered." But chemically, the history of the discovery of silicon has not been easy. Early in the 1800s, most scientists accepted the fact that silicon was an element. However, they had not yet found a way to separate out a sample of pure silicon. The process proved to be more elusive than separating other pure elements.

In the early 1800s, Sir Humphry Davy, an English scientist, came up with a method for separating individual elements from tightly bonded molecules or compounds. He found that if he melted the compounds and then passed an electric current through them, the individual elements in the compound would separate out. This was such an effective method that Davy was able to

English scientist Humphry Davy

separate out sodium, potassium, and calcium from their compounds, producing pure samples of those elements for the first time. But he was unsuccessful in separating out samples of pure silicon.

Around the same time, another attempt to break silicon down was made. In 1811, two French scientists—Joseph Louis Gay-Lussac and Louis Jacques Thenard—gathered samples of silicon tetrachloride, a colorless gas with a very strong odor. They reacted this compound

 What's in a Name?

The terms silica, silicone, and silicon sound alike, but mean very different things. It is not unusual, nor is it accurate, for these terms to be used interchangeably. Here's how to keep them apart:
• silicon is the chemical element with atomic number 14 and chemical symbol of Si;
• silica is a compound made up of silicon and oxygen that is usually white or colorless; it makes up the abundant mineral called quartz;
• silicone is the generic name for a manufactured polymer (a type of plastic) made of silicon and either carbon or oxygen.

Si 14

Silicon

with potassium metal and the result was a very impure form of silicon. However, they weren't given credit for its discovery.

A pure sample of silicon wasn't separated until 1824. Jons Jacob Berzelius, a Swedish chemist from Stock-

Jons Jacob Berzelius is one of two people credited with separating pure silicon.

holm, conducted experiments similar to Davy's original techniques. Berzelius took samples of the compound potassium fluorosilicate, a white crystalline powder, and heated them with melted potassium. The result was a compound made up of potassium silicon fluoride and pure silicon. This product was tainted, but when Berzelius washed it with water, the contaminants were removed and the result was a powdered substance of pure silicon.

Although Berzelius is now credited with discovering pure silicon, he was not the person to name this newly isolated element. Thomas Thomson, a chemist from Scotland, suggested that the new element

Naming Elements

The process for naming newly discovered elements has been complicated and at times controversial. Some were given Latin names. Others were named for legends or folk beliefs (such as thorium for Thor, the Norse god of thunder, right). Still others were named after characters from Greek legends, the places where they were discovered or the scientists involved in their discovery. A few elements were even assigned more than one name, as different scientists could have discovered the element at roughly the same time. In 1947, the International Union of Pure and Applied Chemistry (IUPAC) took over the responsibility for approving a newly discovered element's name and for assigning the symbol for it.

be called silicon. The name comes from *silex*, the Latin word for flint. Thomson's analysis of the element concluded that it was very similar to two other elements, carbon and boron. Therefore, Thomson suggested adding *–on* as an ending to the name, giving us the element *silicon*.

Silicon

Where Silicon Is Found

Silicon is found on and in Earth's crust. Approximately 26 percent of Earth's crust is silicon, second in abundance only to oxygen. Silicon is also found in the Sun and in other stars. Silicon is the eighth most abundant element in the entire universe. It has been identified in the spectral lines from stars, on planets in our solar system and their moons, and in other celestial bodies. For example, **meteorites** called aerolites are composed primarily of silicon. Aerolites, also called stony meteorites, are the most common type of meteorites found on Earth. These meteorites are made up of only a little bit of metal, usually iron, and have a very similar mineral composition to the rocks found on Earth's surface. These minerals are composed largely of silicon. The main difference between aerolites and the rocks found on Earth is the amount of iron they contain. Almost 90 percent of the meteorites found on the ice in Antarctica's glaciers are aerolites.

Recent information sent back to NASA scientists by the Mars Reconnaissance Orbiter allowed them to identify a mineral deposit as a form of silicon. The ground near an ancient, more than 3-billion-year-old volcano on the surface of Mars, contained a **hydrated** form of silica. This led scientists to conclude that there was once a hydrothermal environment on the surface of Mars, meaning there was water on the planet, possibly underground. Scientists see this as one more line of evidence to support the idea that life, in some form, once existed on Mars.

 Silicon on the Moon
While silicon might make up some of the rocks on the Moon's surface, there is even more silicon up there. In 1969, Apollo 11 astronauts Neil Armstrong and Buzz Aldrin left a silicon disc on the surface of the Moon. The disc is about the size of a silver dollar and is placed inside a white pouch. Etched on the disc, in very tiny lettering, are messages of peace and goodwill from 73 different countries.

Si 14
Silicon

At super-hot undersea vents, strange forms of life live, but so far, none are silicon-based.

Silicon and Alien Life?

Science fiction writers and scientists alike have discussed the possibility that alien life forms could be silicon-based. Many point to the fact that life on Earth is carbon-based and silicon and carbon share many of the same properties and characteristics. However, recently, scientists have pointed to some of the particular properties of silicon that make it unlikely to support life. Silicon, when mixed with oxygen in the atmosphere, turns into a solid called silica. This is not conducive to living things. Silicon also does not have a way to store energy. Carbon is able to store energy in the form of carbohydrates, but there is no way for silicon to do likewise. Energy is vital to life, so without a storage capacity, silicon becomes hard to imagine in that role. So, while the idea of a silicon-based life form might work in a novel or movie about space aliens, it just isn't possible.

Text-Dependent Questions

1. What are aerolites?

2. What is the difference between silica, silicone, and silicon?

3. Why is a sample of pure silicon so difficult to find naturally?

Research Project

Find out what rocks are most common in your area. What minerals make up those rocks? Are these minerals silicates?

Making pure silicon

Si 14

Silicon

Chemical Properties

ilicon is not a metal, but it's not a nonmetal, either. It is part of a small group of elements on the periodic table that are classified as **metalloids**. Metalloids have properties that are sometimes similar to those of metals and sometimes of nonmetals. For example, metalloids can conduct heat and electricity, but not as well as a metal can. This property of metalloids, silicon included, gives these elements some unique chemical properties. This particular property creates **semiconductors** (that is, it partially conducts electricity) and has made silicon enormously important in electronics (see Chapter 4).

Silicon is not found by itself in nature. It is always bonded, or joined, with another element or elements. Silicon most

typically forms compounds of silicon dioxide, known as silica. Silica is found in much of Earth's crust in minerals such as quartz, talc, micas, and feldspar. Other minerals composed of silicon are more rare, and, if cut and polished in the right way, are desired as gemstones. These silicon minerals include amethysts, opals, and agates.

Silicon is not only found in the rocks and minerals on Earth's crust, but exists in the water on Earth's surface. It enters into the water in several different ways. The weathering and erosion of rocks on the surface brings silicon-containing minerals into the water. Minerals that are rich in silica, such as quartz, are very resistant to weathering; they don't break down easily. Therefore, they are transported into the bodies of water intact. Volcanic activity also brings silicon into the water supplies. The silicon in water supplies is generally too low to cause any sort of health impact. If it happens to exist at abnormally high concentrations, it has been shown to limit the growth of certain varieties of algae in the water.

At room temperature, silicon exists in two different forms, or allotropes. Allotropes are forms of the same element that have different properties, both chemical and physical. One allotrope of silicon is

A mistake in the lab led to the creation of the heat-oriented Czochralski process.

grayish-black and shiny. It forms into thin, needle-like crystals. The other allotrope has no definite crystalline structure. This form of silicon is usually found as a brown powder.

It is possible to artificially produce a single crystal of silicon in a laboratory setting with a process called the Czochralski process, which was accidentally discovered by a Polish scientist Jan Czochralski in 1915. He was conducting experiments designed to find out more about the rate at which metals crystallize, or turn to a solid. He is rumored to have left a container of molten tin on his table to slowly cool. While he was distracted with his notes, he accidentally dipped his pen into the tin, instead of into the inkwell. Realizing his mistake, he quickly lifted the pen out of the tin to find a thin string of metal hanging from the end of it. This is something that doesn't actually happen in nature—he crystallized a metal by pulling a small sample of it from the surface of a mass of melted metal. The significance of this accidental discovery

was that for the first time, scientists had a way to create single crystals of an element.

The ability to make a single crystal of silicon is very useful, especially in the technology used in electronics. Single crystals of silicon are combined with other elements such as boron, phosphorus, or arsenic to make devices including solar cells, microchips, and transistors.

Other Properties of Silicon

At room temperature, silicon is really an unremarkable element. It doesn't combine with most other elements at this temperature, and things like water or acids can do little to change or alter the element. It does, however, become much more reactive at higher temperatures. When silicon is at temperatures high enough for it to melt (about 2,500°F/1,400°C), it reacts very readily with elements such as oxygen, nitrogen, phosphorus, or sulfur.

Silicon has a few unique physical properties as well. Like water, silicon is denser in the liquid state than it is as a solid. In other words, solid silicon would float in liquid silicon, just as an ice cube floats in a glass of water. Similar to water as well, silicon expands when it freezes. Solid silicon is very brittle and chips easily. It often will crystal-lize into a diamond shape, if given enough space to do so and enough time to cool.

Silicon has three stable isotopes that occur in nature. These are silicon–28, silicon–29, and silicon–30. By far, the most abundant is silicon–28, with just over 92 percent of all silicon in Earth. Twenty

A block of pure, shiny silicon shows clearly that it has metalloid properties.

Si 14
Silicon

radioactive, or unstable, isotopes of silicon have been discovered. The most stable has a half-life of 170 years. This means it takes 170 years for 50 percent of a sample to decay into a different element. Some of the other radioactive isotopes have half-lives of less than seven seconds; however most have a half-life of less than one tenth of a second. These forms of silicon are not around very long at all.

Silicon also forms different alloys. An alloy is a mixture of metals or a mixture of a metal with some other element. In fact, the vast majority of the silicon on Earth, nearly 80 percent of it, is found in the form of ferrosilicon. This is an alloy of iron and silicon with a varying amount of each element. Most of the world's ferrosilicon is found in China. Other leading producers are Russia, Norway, Brazil, and the United States. Primarily, ferrosilicon is used in the iron and steel industries.

From samples of ferrosilicon like this one can come pure silicon.

Text-Dependent Questions

1. How does silicon enter the water?

2. What is an alloy?

3. How is a metalloid like a metal? How is it like a nonmetal?

Research Project

As this chapter pointed out, the accidental discovery by Jan Czochralski in 1915 made the use of silicon in much of our technology possible. Many, many accidental discoveries in science have given us products and technologies that we use every day. Search the Internet to find an example.

Silicon and You

The element silicon has a number of direct impacts on human life. Some are positive, while some can be very negative to human health.

WORDS TO UNDERSTAND

carcinogenic   able to or likely to cause cancer

GRAS   "generally recognized as safe"; a designation assigned by the Food and Drug Administration to chemicals or products that are in contact with humans or their foods

inert   chemically inactive

leach   to move through a membrane from one vessel to another

osteoporosis   a disease of the human skeleton that causes weak or brittle bones

Silicon and Diet

Our bodies contain roughly 1 gram of silicon. This number decreases as we age. Silicon is a requirement in the diets of many organisms, and it is considered necessary in the human diet as well. Silicon in our diets is thought to improve bone health and strength. It is primarily found in the skin and in connective tissues in our bodies. Silicon is found naturally in the plants in our diets. It is recommended that humans take in between 20 and 1,200 milligrams of silicon each day. We can get most of that from the grains we eat. Foods like raisins, brown rice, and green beans contain silicon. Other sources include nuts (right), spinach, and seafood. There is even silicon in the water we drink.

Some people take silicon dietary supplements. They are used primarily as a preventative supplement against **osteoporosis**—a condition that causes weak and brittle bones, often in older people. Limited research has indicated that silicon might have benefits in the prevention or treatment of hair loss, heart disease, digestion problems, or

Alzheimer's disease. Anyone thinking about taking silicon supplements should be sure to consult a doctor before doing so.

Silicon and Your Lungs

Silicosis is a lung disease caused by breathing dust that contains small amounts of crystalline silica. Silicosis can be very debilitating and is often fatal. Crystalline silica is used in concrete, sandstone, rock, paint, or masonry products. The use of power tools for removing paint or rust, blasting or drilling concrete, or demolishing masonry structures can expose workers to dust containing silica. The ultrafine grains of sili-

ca get into the lungs when inhaled. This damages the smallest parts of lungs, making breathing difficult. The most common type of silicosis usually occurs when exposed to very small quantities of the crystalline silica dust for a period of 10 years or more. More-than one million workers in the United States labor in conditions that put them at risk for silicosis. Such work-ers should wear special breathing masks, but, even so, hundreds of people die each year from the disease. The construction industry has one of the highest death rates due to silicosis.

Some silicate minerals have a texture that is fibrous. If disturbed, fibrous minerals can become airborne and enter into the lungs. Microscopic fibrous mineral shards can be-come lodged in the lung tissue, resulting in lung diseases or even lung cancer. One of the more well known examples of **carcinogenic** minerals is asbestos. Not all varieties of

 Deadly Toll

In 1930–31, a hydroelectric plant was constructed in West Virginia. Part of the project involved digging what is known as the Hawk's Nest Tunnel. It took nearly 5,000 workers to dig through Gauley Mountain, near Anstead, West Virginia. More than 760 workers died as a result of silicosis they contracted from this excavation project. Their deaths led to the passage of laws to help work-ers with silicosis.

asbestos are carcinogenic, and even the ones that are need to be disturbed or damaged to be dangerous.

Silicone Bakeware?

Silicone and silicon are not the same thing. Silicon is element 14 on the periodic table. Silicone is a manufactured product, composed of silicon and either carbon or oxygen. Silicone can take several forms—either a solid, liquid, or a gel-like substance. Silicone is used in medical implants or devices like pacemakers. It has also found a use in bakeware like muffin tins, spatulas, and candy molds. Silicone bakeware is flexible, can be transferred from the freezer to a very hot oven, and is nonstick. It seems to be the perfect product, but questions arise about its safety for humans who use it.

The Food and Drug Administration examined silicone in the 1970s and found that silicon dioxides (of which silicone is one) were generally recognized as safe. This **GRAS** designation from the FDA says that the substance is "shown to be safe under the conditions of its intended use." It should be noted, however, that silicone bakeware and spatulas didn't become available on the mass market until a decade later. The FDA has not done any other studies on silicone since the 1970s.

The research on either the harmful or the non-harmful effects to humans has been limited. It has been suggested that silicone is essentially **inert**, and stable, so it does not react with food nor does it **leach** chemicals into the food or release vapors. There has been some concern raised about the stability of the products at very high temperatures, those which exceed the recommended usage. It has been suggested, however, that people who are sensitive to chemicals in general may want to avoid silicone bakeware until the research is more conclusive.

Si
Silicon
14

Silicon Combines

Silicon is not found in a pure state in nature. It is always found in combination with other elements. On Earth, the most common element that silicon is found with is oxygen, creating silicon dioxide, or silica. The mineral quartz is made of silicon dioxide. In fact, quartz is one of the most common minerals in Earth's crust. Silicon forms many different compounds. It combines easily with elements like magnesium, calcium, and phosphorus. However, two of the most common types of compounds are silicates and oxides.

Silicates

A silicate is a compound that has an atom of silica bonding with another element. Most of the time, that element is

oxygen, although in some cases silica can bond with fluoride to form hexasilicates.

Silicates that contain oxygen make up nearly 90 percent of the minerals and rocks in Earth's crust. Mercury, Mars, and Venus as well as rocky moons and some asteroids are made of silicates. Minerals such as quartz, mica, feldspar, and talc are all silicates. Consider the properties and uses of some of the more common or well-known silicate minerals.

Garnets: Garnets are usually composed of magnesium or calcium along with aluminum, silicon, and oxygen. Garnets are found in all rock types: sedimentary, igneous, and metamorphic rocks. This is because they are very durable and resistant to heat. Most of us know of garnet as a reddish gemstone (specifically as

Bright red garnets are often found in jewelry . . . for January!

January's birthstone). However, there are many other different colors of garnet—green, yellowish, or orange—and it has some very practical uses. Because it is such a durable and strong silicate mineral, garnet is often used as an abrasive in manufacturing, as the abrasive in sandpaper for carpentry and woodworking, or is used a cutting mechanisms for ceramics or stone.

Talc: This is the softest mineral on the **Mohs's cale of hardness**. Talc is a silicate mineral made of magnesium, silicon, and oxygen. It is commonly known, when crushed into a fine powder, as talcum powder. While it is true that talc is used in body powders and cosmetics, it also has many other uses. Talc is used in manufacturing plastics and for making ceramic tiles, pottery, dinnerware, and paint. Talc is also now included in the organic fiber pulp that is used to make paper. Talc not only can improve the brightness and whiteness of the paper but also helps improve the paper's ability to absorb ink.

Zircon: The very durable silicate mineral composed of silicon, zirconium, and oxygen is called zircon. Zircon is a common gemstone, known for its varied and bright colors and durability. Zircons are used as the primary ore for the element zirconium, which is used to make

Silicon Carbide

Silicon carbide, or carborundum, as it is sometimes referred to, is another very important compound of silicon. Carborundum has a hardness of about 9.5 on the Mohs' scale, making it one of the hardest known substances. Not only is it very hard but it also can withstand very high temperature. It does so by reflecting, rather than absorbing,

Silicon carbide bits cover these sanding tubes, used for grinding and polishing.

heat. This makes it a refractory material. These two properties have given silicon carbide a variety of practical applications, including use as an abrasive to grind or polish other materials and to line the inside of ovens where very high temperatures are needed.

Caroborundum is also used as a synthetic gemstone known as moissanite. Moissanite is very similar to diamond; it has a similar hardness and similar optical qualities. Moissanite is harder than cubic zirconium and is popular as a diamond substitute in engagement rings and other jewelry.

Silicon in Alloys

One of the most significant uses of silicon is in the production of **alloys**. An alloy is a mixture of metals or of a metal with a different element. Alloys that include silicon are made with metal elements such iron, aluminum, and copper. During the production of silicon, iron is often added to the furnace during the process. The result is an alloy called ferrosilicon. That alloy is used to improve the strength and durability of steel or can be used to remove impurities from steel during the manufacturing process.

Campers in these tents can thank silicone for keeping the rain from getting in.

and other products to add shine, strength, and conditioning to the hair and skin.

Fabrics: Tents and outdoor clothing are now made with a coating of silicone. This added silicone makes the fabric breathable as well as resistant to the elements. Other clothing benefits from added silicone that helps reduce wrinkles, making iron-free fabrics.

Medical devices: Many of the devices used today in the medical field are made of silicone, including catheters, surgery tape, and dressings used to help minimize scarring.

Solar power: Silicone is making the solar power industry a reality for many more people and applications. Silicone is stable in the presence of ultraviolet radiation and it is very durable. Silicone-based solar panels have electrical insulating properties and are resistant to moisture.

Windows: Work is being done now to produce a better window by introducing silicone into the process. These new windows would be more energy efficient by allowing the user to transform the glass from transparent to opaque, allowing people in the room to decide what the heating, cooling, and lighting needs are.

 Text-Dependent Questions

1. What is a silicate mineral? Give two examples.

2. How is silicone used in solar panels?

3. List the steps of how silicone is made.

Research Project

What products in your home or your medicine cabinet contain silicon? Research the ingredients of at least five different products to find out if there is a silica compound in them. Make a list and be sure to include all the ingredients.

Si 14
Silicon

Silicon in Our World

Remember the window you looked through in the Introduction? It was probably made of glass, which means you were looking through silicon. The glass that is such an important part of your life is made from melted silicon. From the windows in your home, to the glasses you use for drinking, to the lenses you use to read the words on the page—all of these different forms of glass were made in very similar fashion. The main ingredient in all glass is silicon, in the form of silica sand. Silica sand melts at temperatures of about 3,000°F (1,700°C). When mixed with other things like soda ash and limestone, the melting point is lowered to about 2,400°F (or 1,300°C). The glassmaking process not only involves high temperatures, but also takes a lot of time. It

Si 14

Silicon

takes roughly 20 hours for the mixture of silicon, soda ash, and limestone to become glass, and it must be stirred during the final hours. It takes about 700 pounds (318 kg) of sand to make 600 pounds (272 kg) of glass.

Silica sand is mixed with additives at the beginning of the process. Additives like sodium carbonate (or washing soda) are added to lower the temperature. Without the additive, it would be necessary to heat the sand to temperatures upwards of 4,172°F/2,300°C (the melting point of quartz). The added sodium carbonate significantly reduces that melting temperature to make the process easier on a commercial level. The problem with that, however, is that with the added sodium carbonate, water can pass through the resulting glass. Another additive, such as calcium oxide, is added to stop that from happening. Glass can be made more

Glass can be heated and shaped by master craftspeople.

durable with the addition of things like magnesium oxide or aluminum oxide. The additives are important but usually only account for about one-third of the whole mixture.

The mixture of sand and additives is added to a container that can reach temperatures of 2,732°F to 4,532°F (1,500 to 2,500°C).

 Fulgurites

Regular beach sand is made up of the mineral quartz, which contains silicon. If lightning happens to strike sand, the result is a form of glass called a fulgurite. Lightning strikes have enough energy to melt the silicon in the sand. It cools very rapidly after the strike, forming small, tube-like pieces of glass. Fulgurite is very fragile but can form into beautiful shapes.

Silicon 14

The mixture is then melted into a liquid in a **kiln** or gas-fired furnace. The mixture must be mixed or agitated to remove bubbles from the liquid and to ensure that it has a consistent thickness and texture.

Once melted, the liquid glass can be poured into a mold or turned into windowpanes. They are made by pouring the melted glass into melted tin and then spraying it with nitrogen gas, which helps shape the glass as it cools. The process of cooling is called annealing. This is done slowly so that points of stress within the glass can be removed. Glass that hasn't been cooled this way tends to be brittle or fragile.

Depending on the ultimate end use of the glass, other materials can be added to give the glass a certain color or specific properties. For example, uranium is sometimes added to the mixture to give glass a fluorescent yellow or green color. Iron oxide and chromium may be added to make glass green, and decorative blue glass is formed by adding cobalt to the sand mixture before it is melted.

Silicon in Living Things

Only a very few organisms use silicon directly in either their structure or within their systems. Three organisms that do are diatoms,

Diatoms and other radiolaria are tiny plants that rely on silicon for life.

radiolaria, and certain types of sponges. Diatoms are a type of unicellular algae. Radiolaria are protozoa, or animal-like **unicellular** organisms. These two organisms, along with certain sponges, have a form of silicon called biogenic silica in their skeletons. This form of silicon is better known as the semiprecious stone called opal.

Certain plants rely on silicon as part of their cell structure or to help with growth. For example, rice plants rely on silicon to help them grow. Much research has been focused on silicon's role in strength of the cell walls of plants and the ability to use this to the maximum benefit to humans. Breeding experiments are underway to study the role of silicon in plant structure and how it might help enhance a plant's ability to resist drought, frost, pests, or certain diseases. Silicon also helps the growth of plant roots and increases the amount of biomass certain crop plants produce.

Si 14
Silicon

Semiconductors

Silicon is a semiconductor, a substance that can conduct an electric current. We are able to change and control the conductivity of semiconductors, which makes them very useful in the manufacturing of the chips and circuits essential for computers, cell phones, and other electronic devices.

This stack of silicon wafers can be sliced up into tiny chips to power electronics.

Most semiconductors are made of silicon. A crystal made of pure silicon has very high insulating properties—this means that very little electricity will flow through it. But it is possible to change the behavior of silicon into a substance that will allow electricity to flow through it. This is done with a process called **doping**, which happens when a small impurity is mixed into the crystal of silicon. This is done by adding elements such as phosphorus, arsenic, boron, or gallium to the silicon crystal. The result is a crystal with small gaps in the structure that are surrounded by a positive change. Since electricity is the flow of electrons, or negative charges, electricity can flow through those small gaps. This changes the function

Silicon Valley

Silicon Valley is an area in northern California known for the large number of silicon chip manufacturers and developers, high tech corporations, and scientific development.  It earned its famous name in 1971. Don Hoefler, a columnist for a publication called *Electronic News*, was working on a story about the semiconductor industry that was growing in the San Francisco area. Hoefler was at lunch one day with people from one of the companies and overheard one of the marketing personnel refer to "Silicon Valley." He liked that title so much that in his next story the headline read "Silicon Valley, USA."

Si 14
Silicon

of the silicon crystal from an insulator to a material that can conduct electricity. However, the electric current is not conducted as well as it is with other substances, which is why it is only called a *semi*conductor.

Solar Cells

The same properties that make silicon a logical choice for use in semiconductors make it a logical choice of material for solar panel technology. Silicon solar cells are built with added impurities in the

Silicon is a key part of solar cells that help turn sunlight into electricity.

crystals of silicon. They increase the ability of the silicon crystal to conduct electricity. In this case, the added impurities are atoms of the element phosphorus and boron.

Doping with phosphorus creates an overall negative charge on the crystals, while doping with boron gives the crystals an overall positive charge. When these two different types of silicon crystals interact, they create an electric field.

Construction Materials

Silicon, or more accurately, natural materials that contain silicon, are unique in that they are largely used in their pure form. There is little processing required when using materials like crushed stone or sand that is rich in silicon minerals such as quartz or feldspar. Construction materials such as clay and sand have many applications. Silicon-based materials are used as a main ingredient in one of the most widely used types of cements in the world. Portland cement is the basic ingredient for building materials such as concrete, mortar, and stucco. Most varieties of Portland cement are between 20–25 percent silica dioxide.

Silicon

Quartz Watches

Certain minerals, including quartz, will take on an interesting property when squeezed: They conduct electricity. In other words, electricity can pass through the crystal. Or, if electricity is passed through the crystal, the crystal will vibrate back and forth. This is a phenomenon called **piezoelectricity**.

One way to think of this property is to think of it as a battery. The crystal of quartz essentially becomes a battery with a positive charge on one side and a negative charge on the other; this is created as the electricity flows through it.

Watches or clocks that operate with piezoelectric quartz crystals are able to keep time very precisely. For this application, the electricity isn't generated by the quartz, but is passed through the quartz to make it vibrate. Electric energy from a battery is passed through the crystal, making it vibrate thousands of times each second. This vibration is slowed down and passed through a motor and the gears to move them once every second.

Piezoelectric technology is also used in devices such as ultrasound equipment, microphones, and ink jet printers.

Silicon went into the glass on this watch face and into the tiny parts inside.

Fused Quartz

Fused quartz is a type of glass made from amorphous silica. Amorphous silica has no definite crystalline structure. This is different from the other types of glass because there are no impurities added to lower the melting temperature. It can, therefore, be used and manipulated at very high temperatures. The resulting glass is very pure and is very strong.

Fused quartz is used in products like halogen lamps, which heat to very high temperatures. Fused quartz is also used in memory chips that are able to store data even if the power is suddenly shut off. But it is possible to erase the memory from the chip when exposed to a very strong ultraviolet light. The mirrors in telescopes are made from fused quartz due to its superior optical properties. And modern glass

Si 14

Silicon

instruments, such as the glass harp, the verrophone, and the glass harmonica, are now being made from fused quartz.

Silicon is found in nearly 90 percent of all the minerals on Earth's surface and is probably one of the most underappreciated elements on the periodic table. Most of us don't realize the role that silicon plays in our everyday lives—from the technology that makes our cell phones

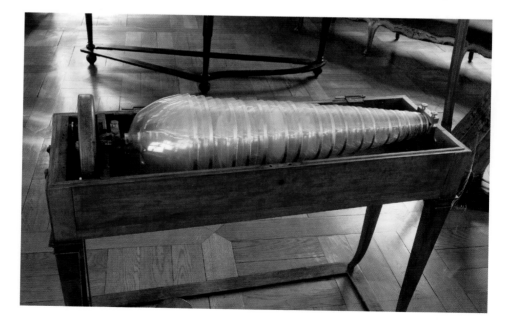

The glass harmonica has a series of bowls that are touched and played as they spin.

operate, to the beach sand that gets inside our shoes and socks, to the advances in solar power that heat and light our world, and to the colorful gemstones that may adorn our fingers—silicon is all around us.

How glass is made

Text-Dependent Questions

1. What is a fulgurite?

2. Name an animal that depends on silicon.

3. How does silicon help in large building projects?

Research Project

Look more into how glass is made. See if you can come up with a list of five different types of glass made from silicon.

FIND OUT MORE

Books

Hantula, Richard. *How Do Solar Panels Work?* New York, NY: Chelsea Clubhouse, 2009.
The parts and technology behind solar panels rely on the use of silicon. Find out how solar panels work and the role of silicon here in this book!

Lauf, Robert J. *Collector's Guide to Quartz and Other Silica Minerals*. Atglen, PA: Schiffer Publishing, 2012.
Think you might want to start collecting some of the beautiful rocks and minerals made up of silicon? This guide is a great place to start!

Shueh, Sam. *Silicon Valley*. New York, NY. Arcadia Publishing, 2009.
Check out some images from the early days in Silicon Valley in this book.

Websites

www.britglass.org.uk/about-glass
Glass is everywhere. Find out more about the amazing world of glass here.

www.dowcorning.com/content/discover/
Dow Corning is one of the world's leading manufacturers of silicone. Explore the various uses and forms of silicone on its website.

www.cdc.gov/niosh/docs/2004-108/pdfs/2004-108.pdf
The Centers for Disease Control has put out an informational guide about silicosis. Read it here.

SERIES GLOSSARY OF KEY TERMS

carbohydrates a group of organic compounds including sugars, starches, and fiber

conductivity the ability of a substance for heat or electricity to pass through it

inert unable to bond with other matter

ion an atom with an electrical charge due to the loss or gain of an electron

isotope an atom of a specific element that has a different number of neutrons; it has the same atomic number but a different mass

nuclear fission process by which a nucleus is split into smaller parts, releasing massive amounts of energy

nuclear fusion process by which two atomic nuclei combine to form a heavier element while releasing energy

organic compound a chemical compound in which one or more atoms of carbon are linked to atoms of other elements (most commonly hydrogen, oxygen, or nitrogen)

solubility the ability of a substance to dissolve in a liquid

spectrum the range of electromagnetic radiation with respect to its wavelength or frequency; can sometimes be observed by characteristic colors or light

INDEX

Photo Credits

Dreamstime.com: Jacek Chabraszewski 7, Manfredxy 10, Tracy Hebden 12, Philip Maguire 17, Benoit Daoust 22, Lasse Kristensen 31, Kelpfish 32, Deymos 34, Luca Petruzzi 38, Jamey Elkins 40, Daniel127001 41, Looman 42, Flashon Studio 46, Elena Elisseva 48, Alexei Novikov 50, Farbled 51, Maryna Konoplytska 53, Aleksej Penkov 54, Zimmytws 55, nh77 56, Kellydt 58. NASA/JPL: 36. Shutterstock: Blueringmedia 8, Bjoern Wylezich 27. Wikimedia: 14, 16, Sharon Moore 19, 25, 28, 60.

About the Author

Jane P. Gardner has written more than 30 books for young and young-adult readers on science and other nonfiction topics. She authored the *Science 24/7* series as well as several titles in the *Black Achievements in Science* series. In addition to her writing career, she also has years of classroom teaching experience. Jane taught middle school and high school science and currently teaches chemistry at North Shore Community College in Massachusetts. She lives in eastern Massachusetts with her husband and two sons.